FRUITS & FLOWERS
A COLORING BOOK

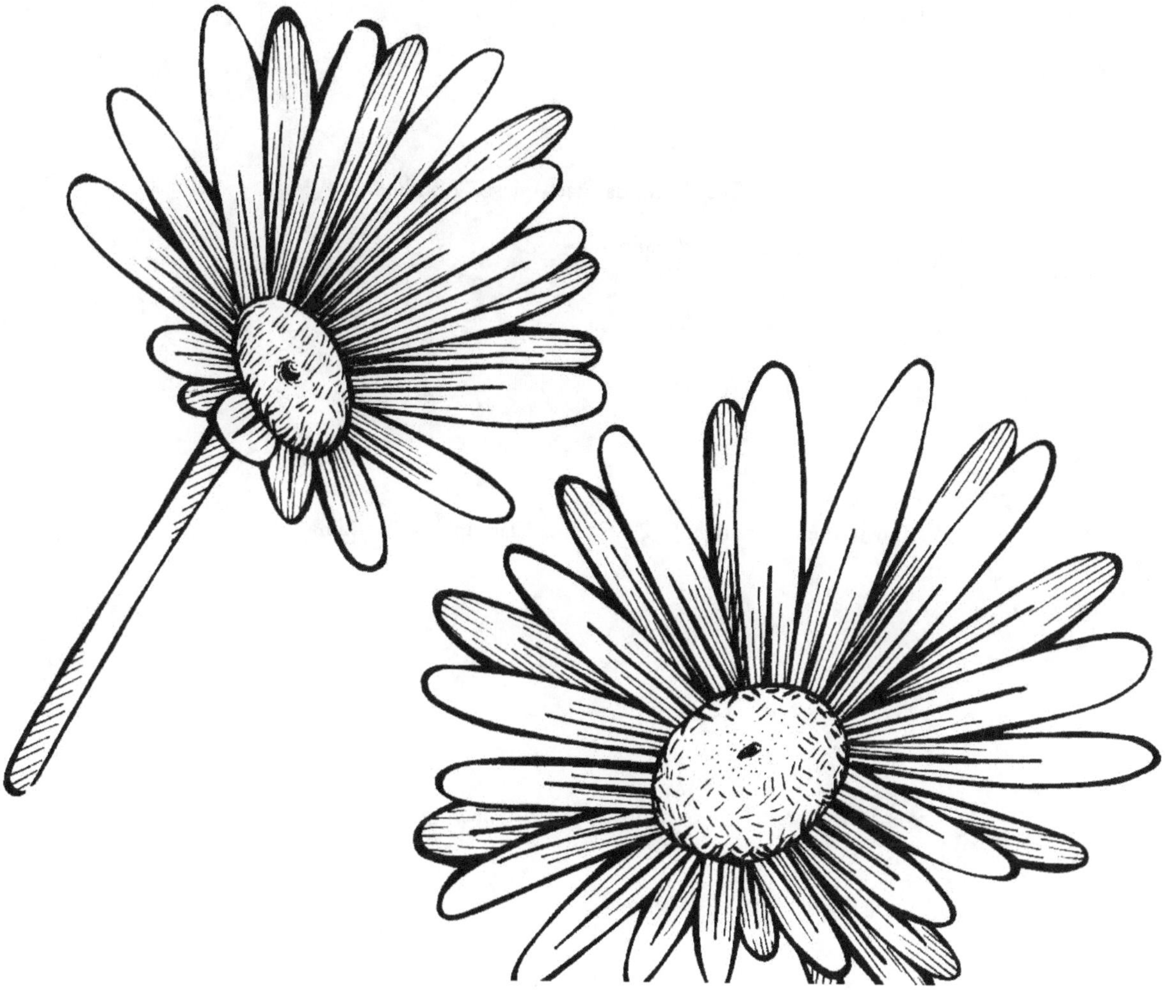

ILLUSTRATIONS BY
M.C. IGLESIAS

Cover Illustration: *Tiger-lily* by M.C. Iglesias (Clara Iglesias-Rondina)

Coloring Books Series – Volume 1

CreateSpace, Charleston, SC, 2015

ISBN: 1514802848
ISBN-13: 978-1514802847

To my siblings Fabiana and Juan Manuel

CONTENTS

FRUITS

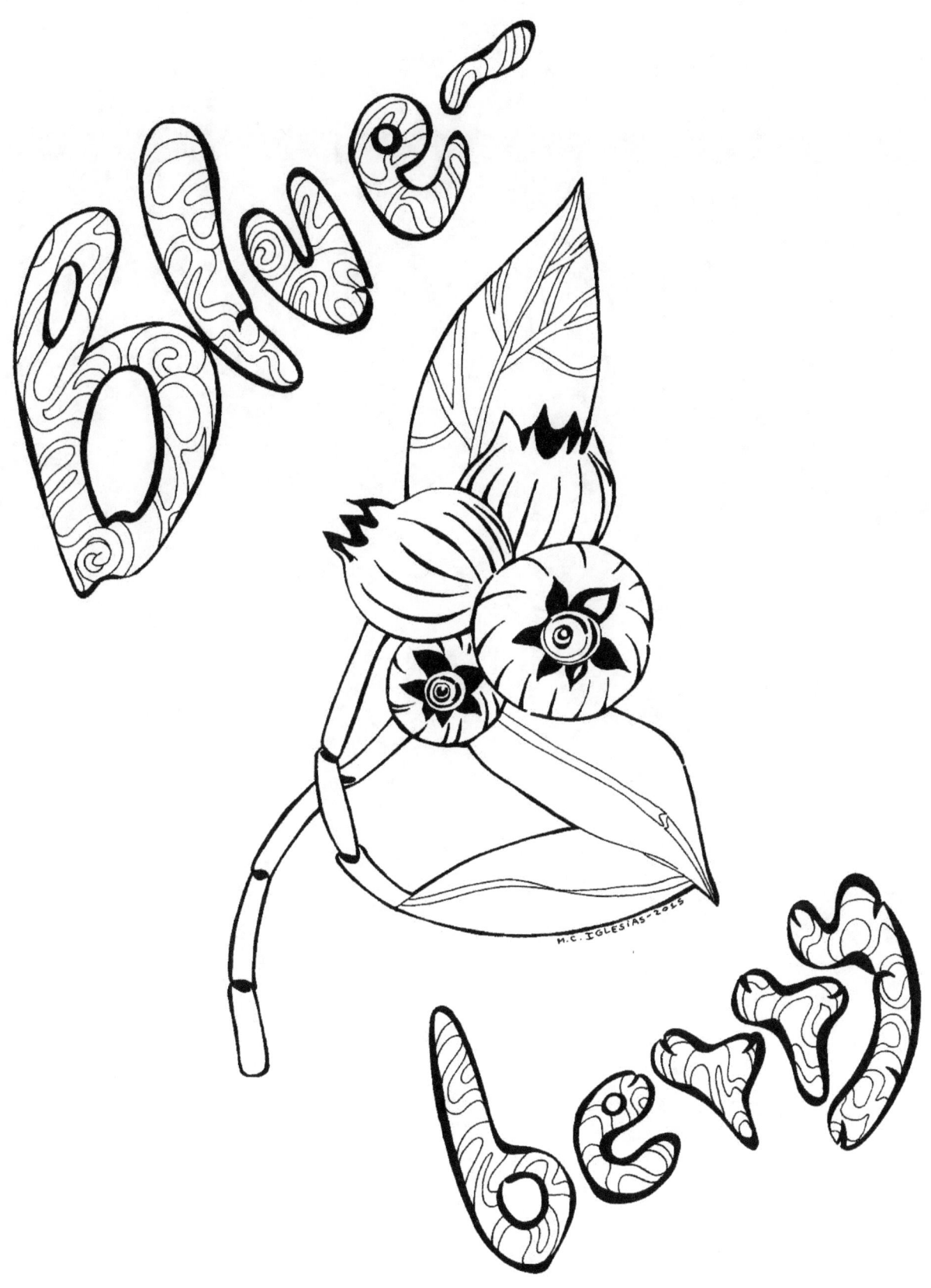

BLUEBERRY *(VACCINIUM CYANOCOCCUS)*

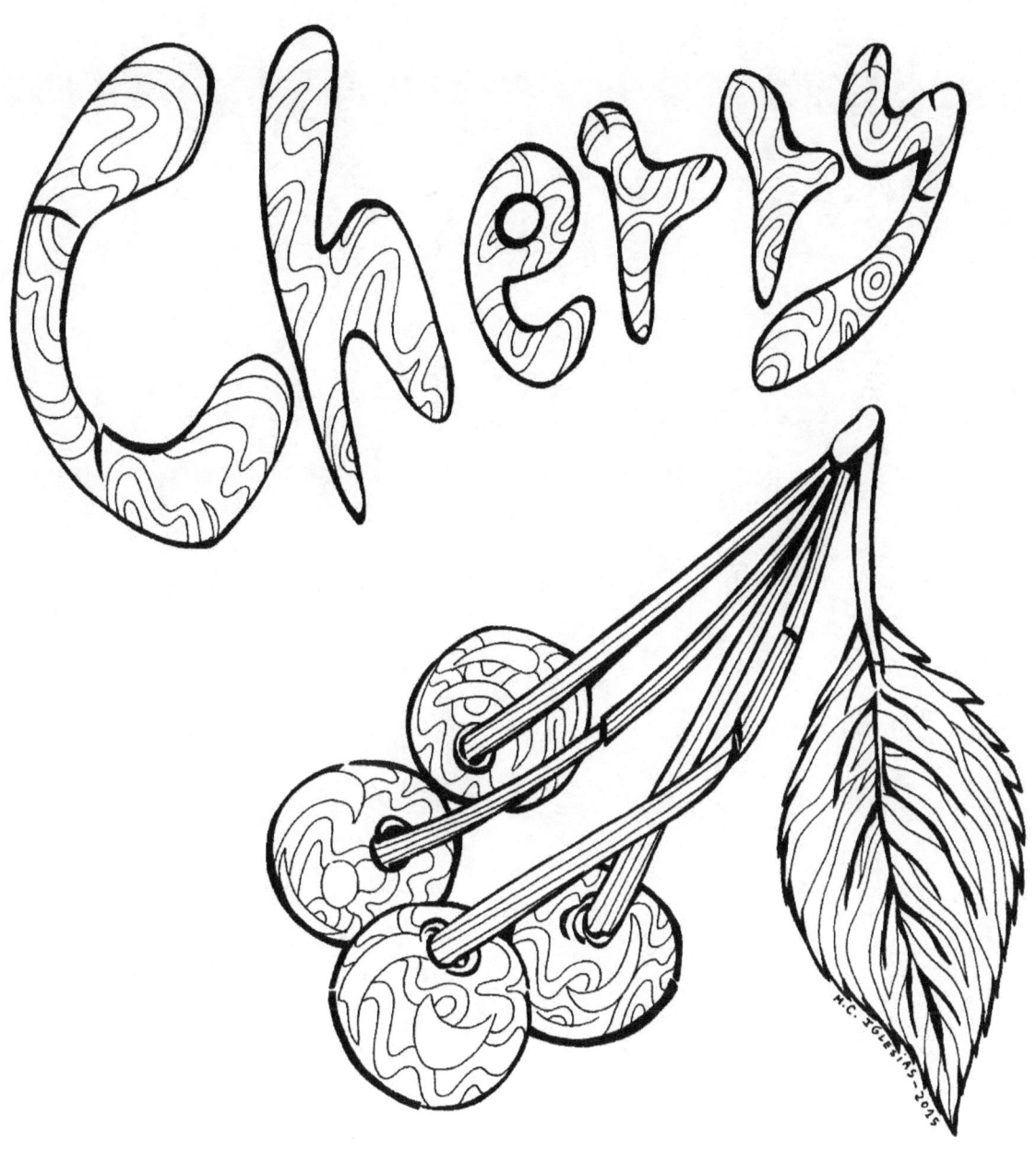

CHERRY *(PRUNUS AVIUM)*

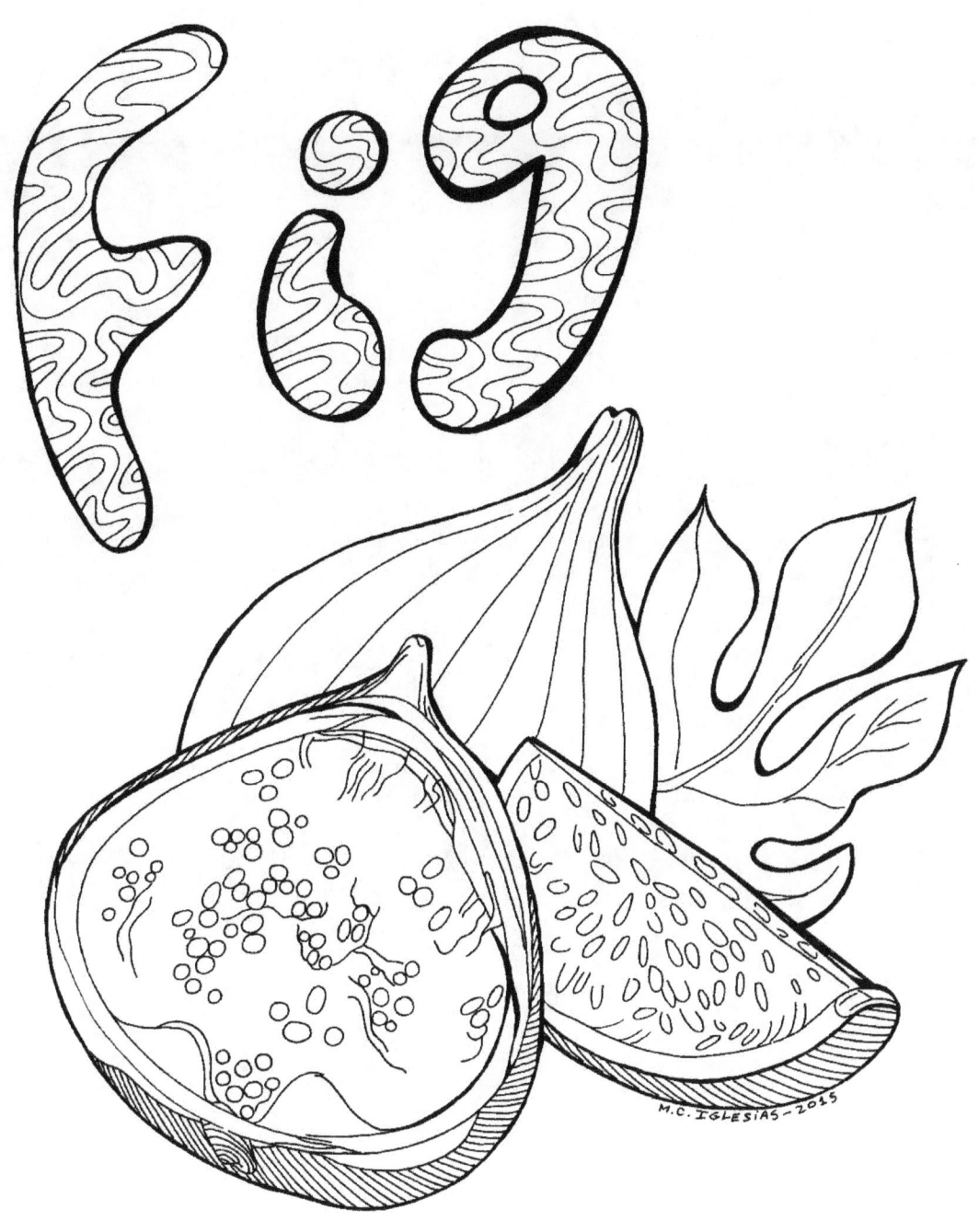

FIG *(FICUS CARICA)*

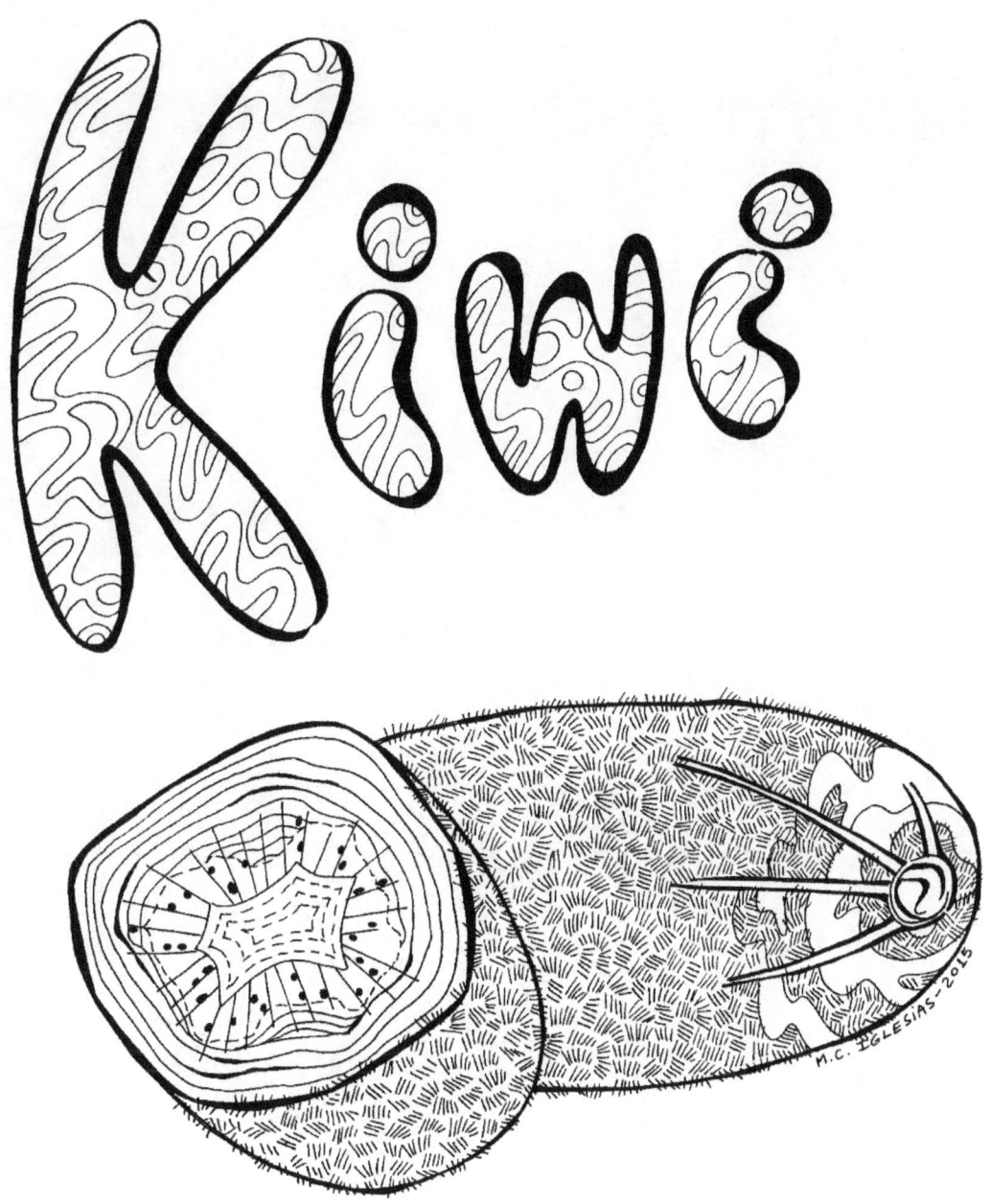

KIWI *(ACTINIDIA DELICIOSA)*

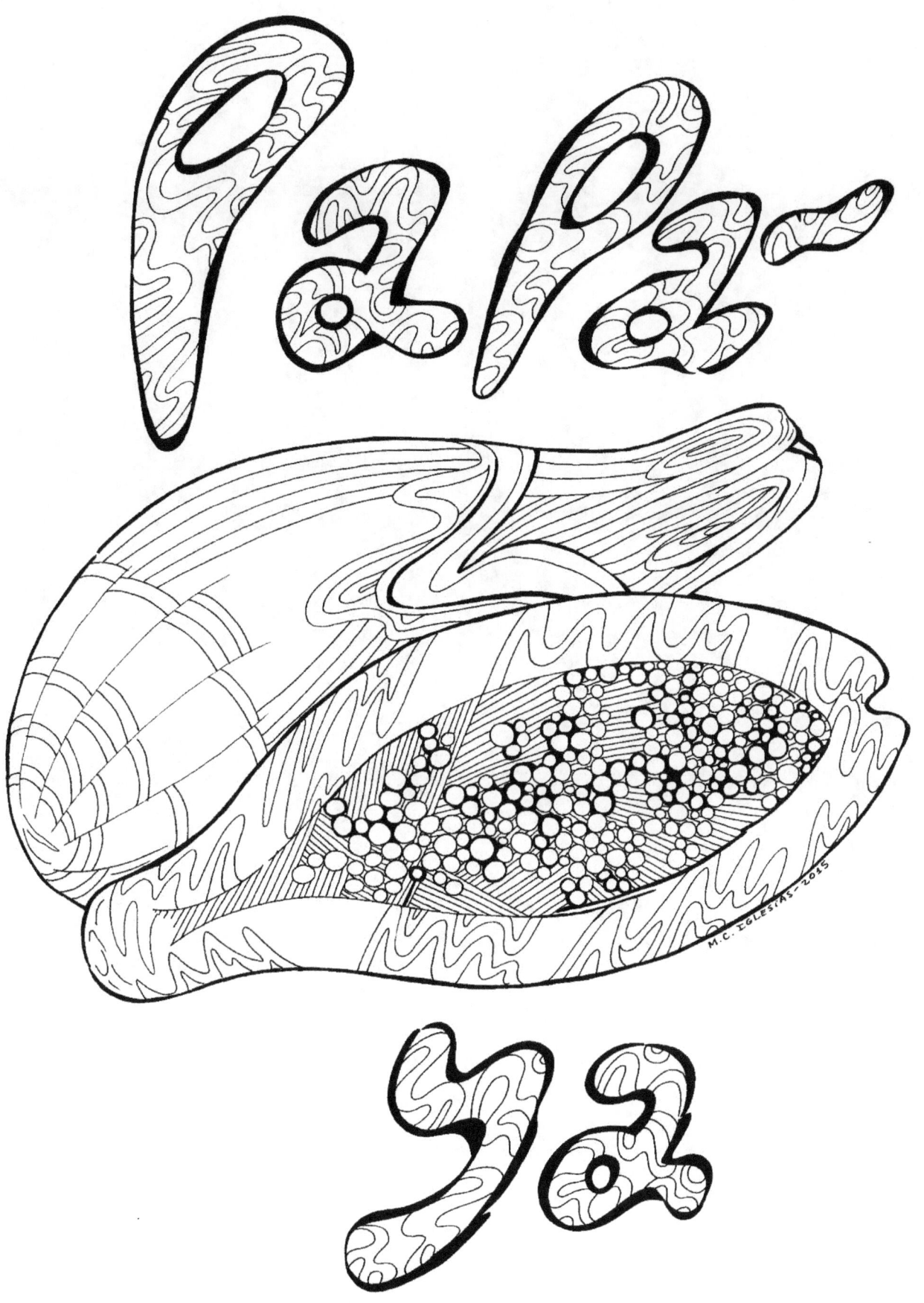

PAPAYA *(CARICA PAPAYA)*

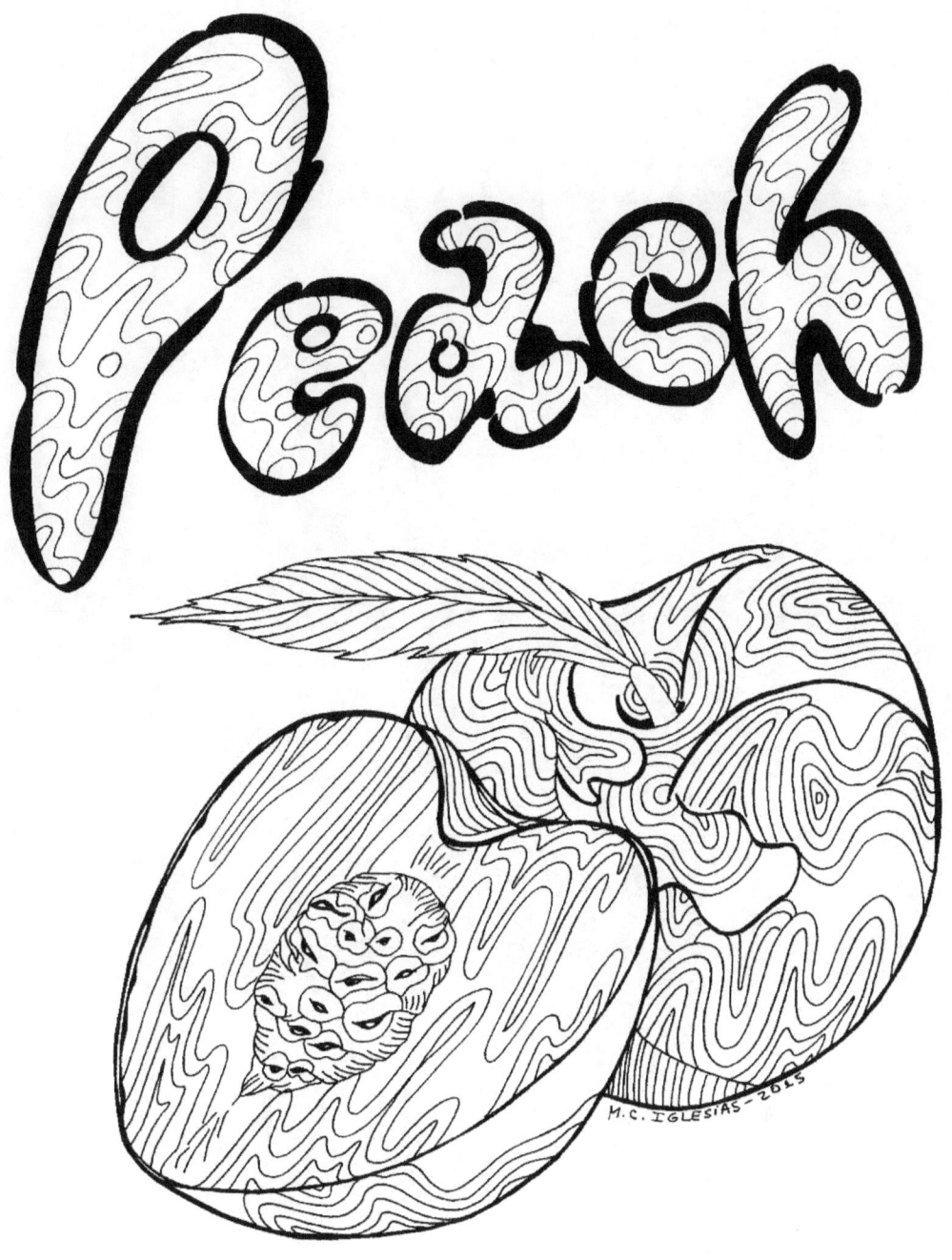

PEACH *(PRUNUS PERSICA)*

FRUITS & FLOWERS. A COLORING BOOK

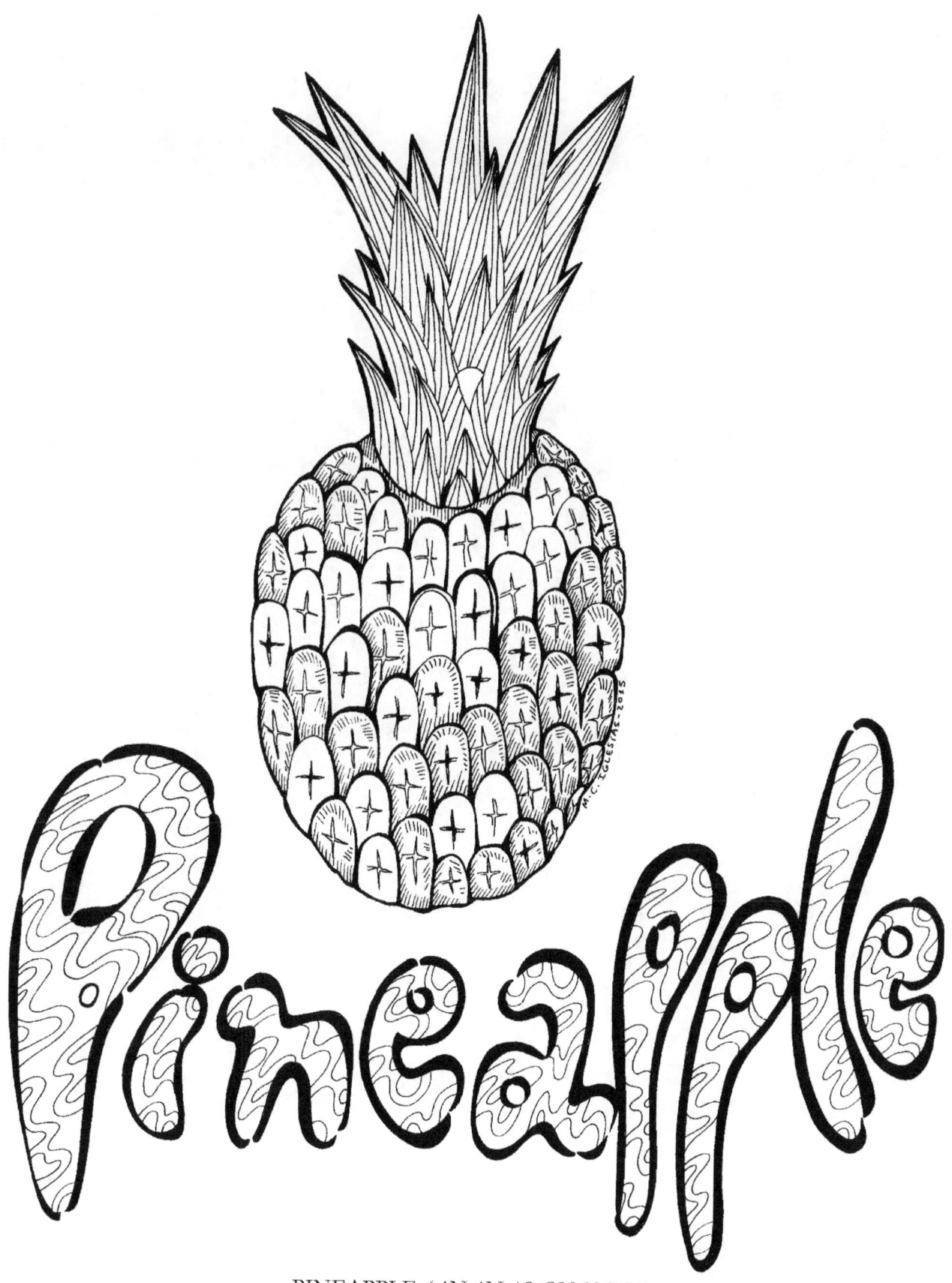

PINEAPPLE *(ANANAS COMOSUS)*

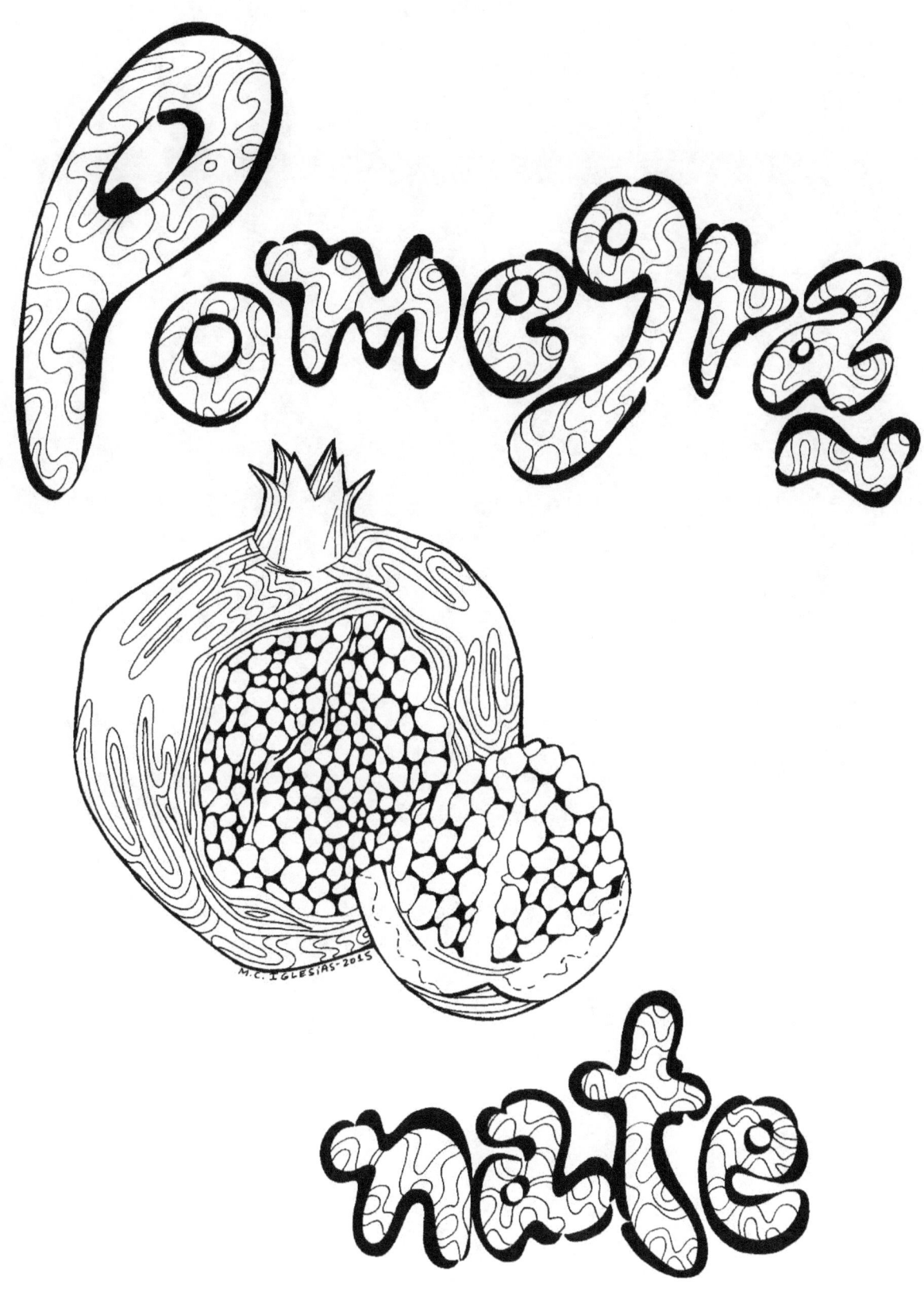

POMEGRANATE *(PUNICA GRANATUM)*

24

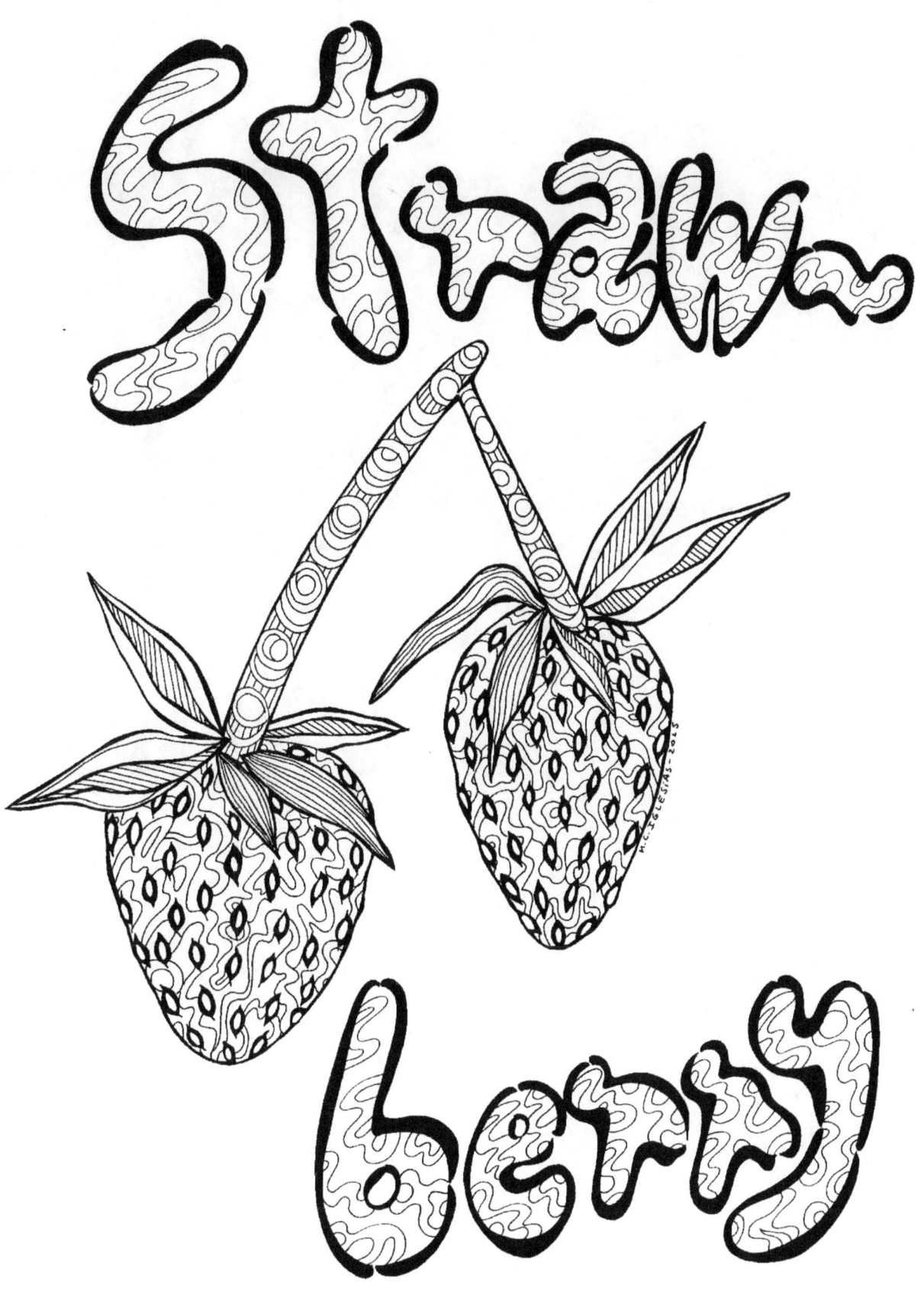

STRAWBERRY (FRAGARIA ANANASSA)

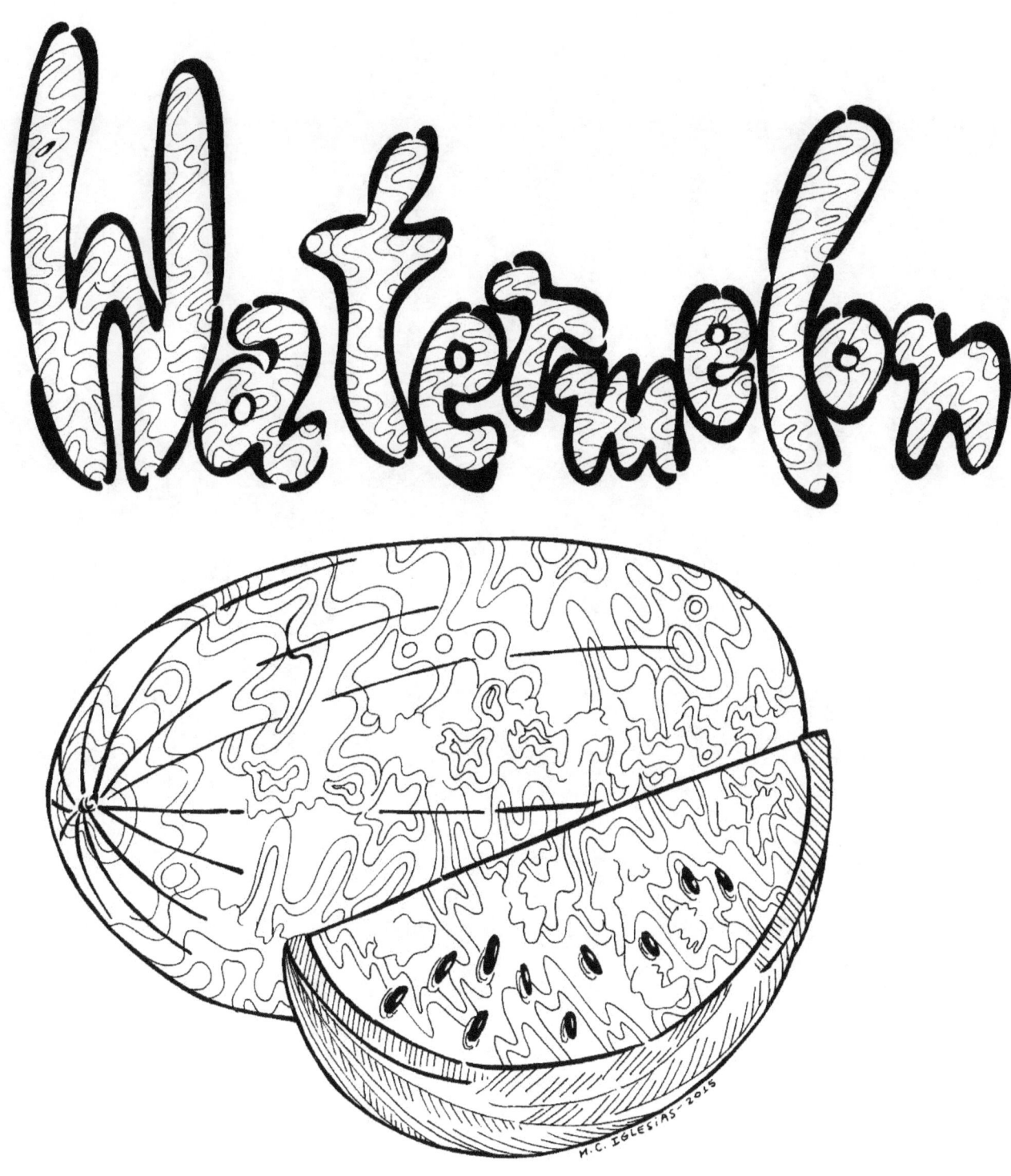

WATERMELON (*CITRULLUS LANATUS*)

FRUITS & FLOWERS. A COLORING BOOK

FLOWERS

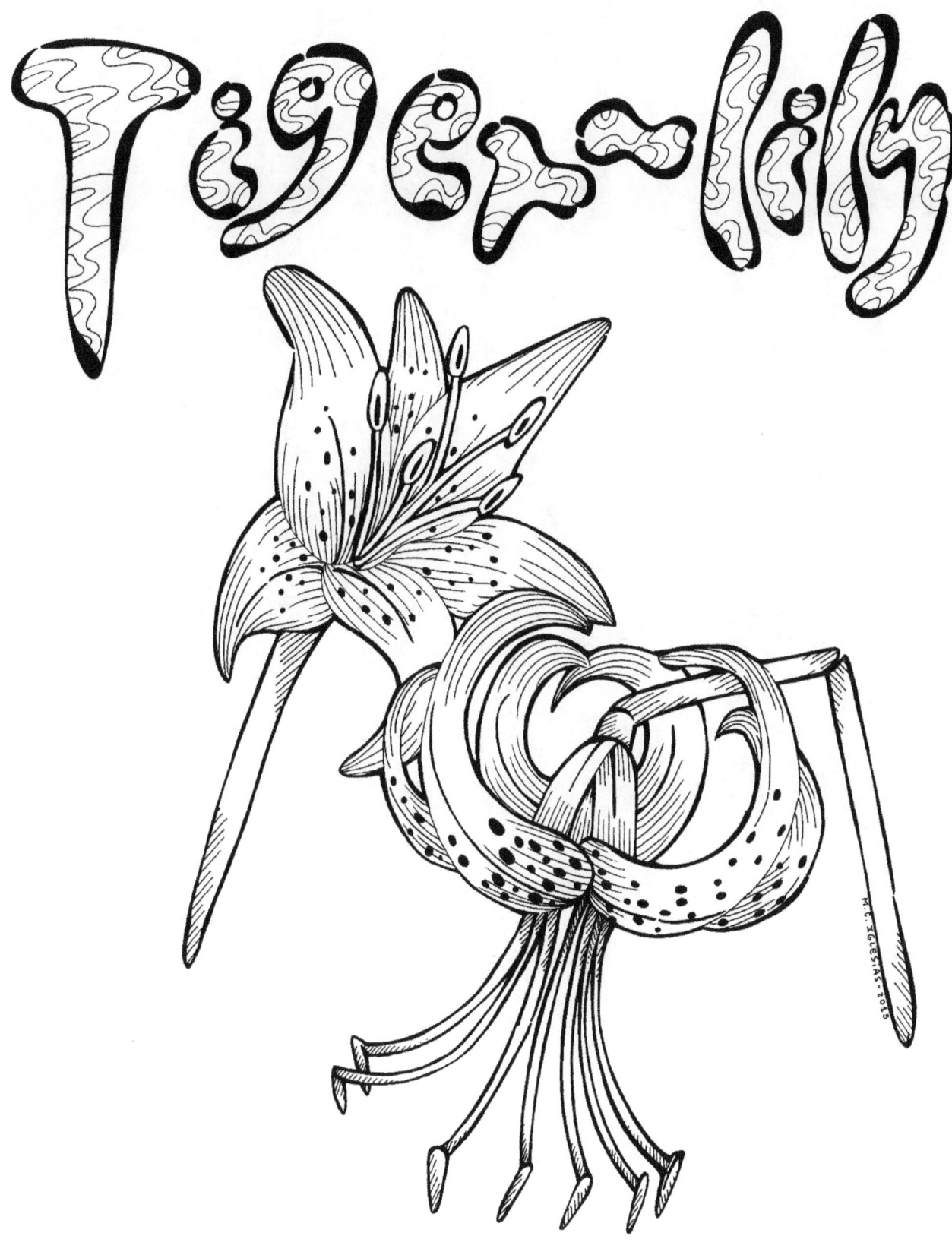

TIGER-LILY *(LILIUM COLUMBIANUM)*

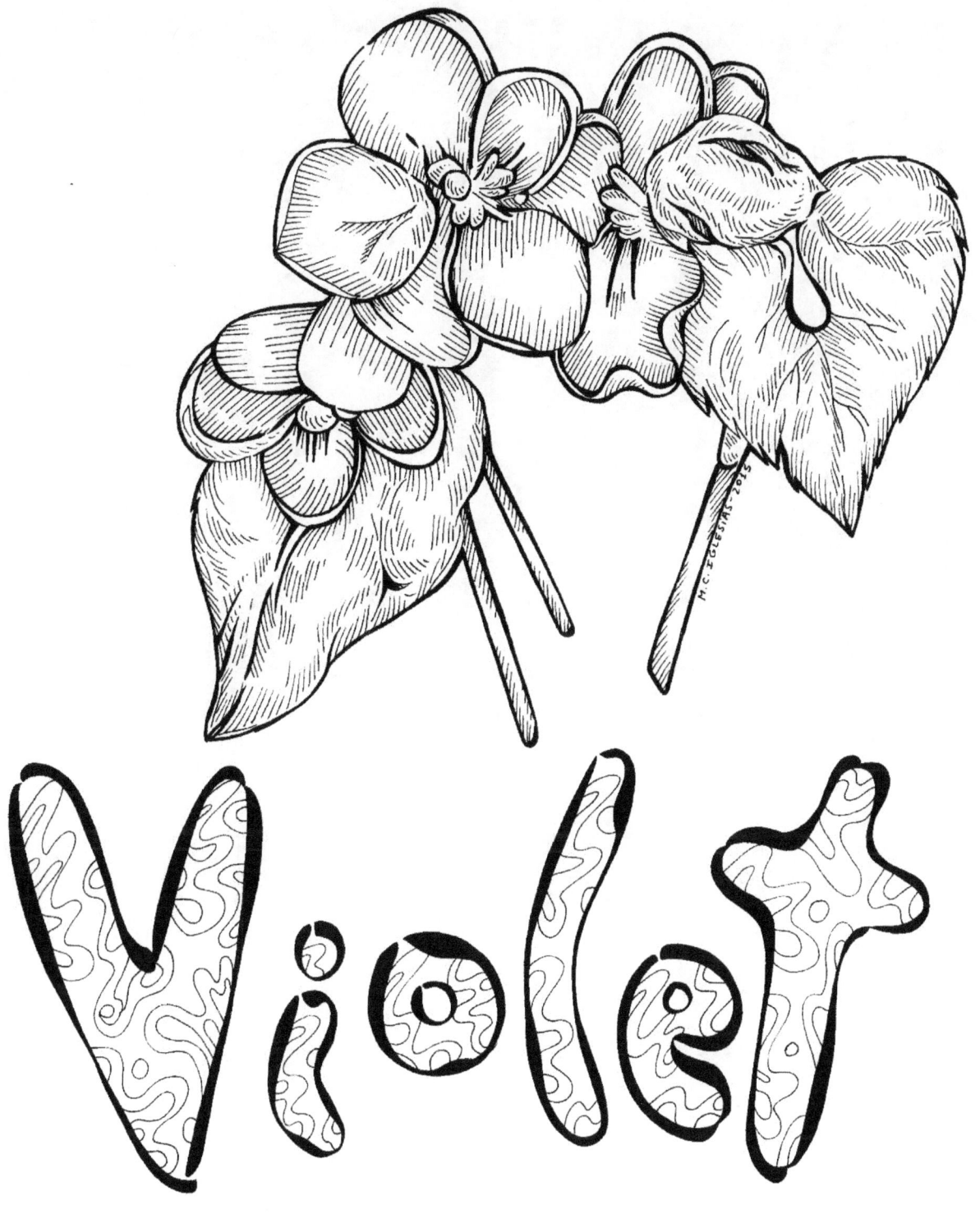

VIOLET *(VIOLA ODORATA)*

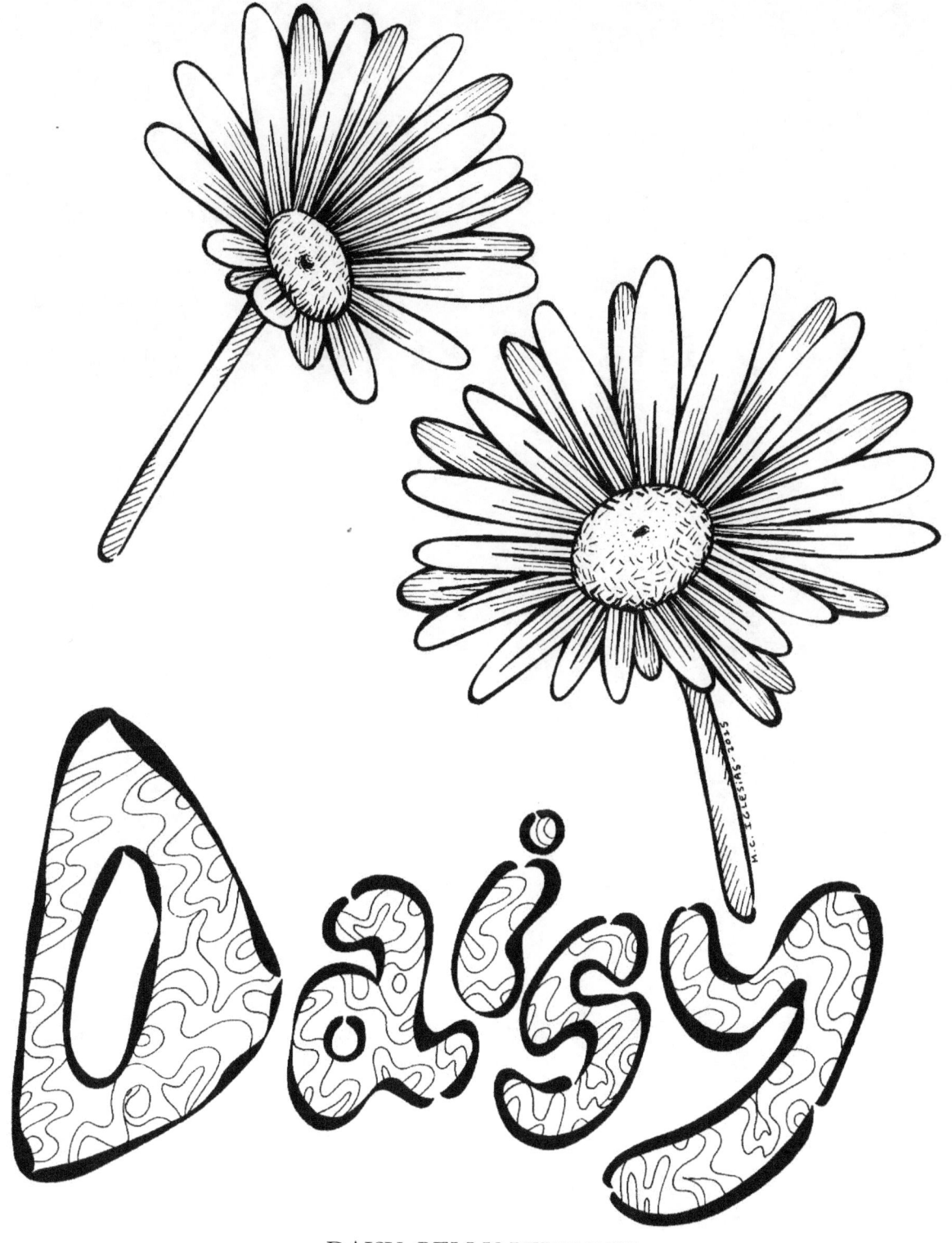

DAISY *(BELLIS PERENNIS)*

ABOUT THE AUTHOR AND HER WORK

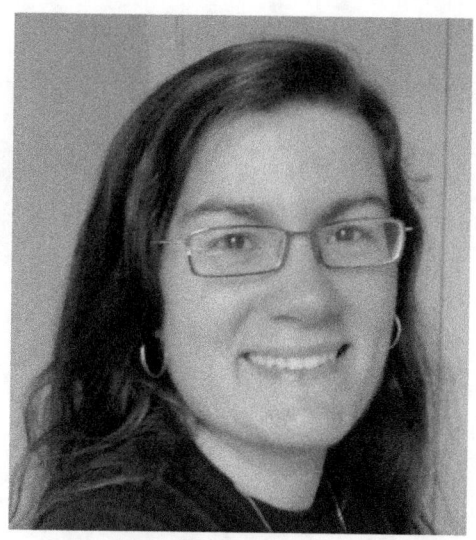

M.C. Iglesias (Clara Iglesias-Rondina) is an illustrator, scholar and author. Born in Argentina, she earned her Ph.D. in Italian Studies at Yale University, specializing in medieval and early modern thought. Prior to Yale she obtained a B.A. and M.A. at the Complutense University of Madrid, Spain, as well as a B.F.A at the Art School of Santa Fe, Argentina. She has participated in solo and collective exhibits in Argentina and the U.S., winning several awards in recognition for her artworks. In addition, she has different academic publications on authors such as Dante Alighieri, Jorge Luis Borges, or Niccolò Machiavelli.

Fruits & Flowers. A Coloring Book is an unusual coloring book conceived to be used by adults (in particular senior citizens) and children. Each of its thirteen illustrations represents a fruit or flower accompanied by its English name to be colored as well. In this way an association is built between the form depicted and its denomination. This could constitute a valuable exercise in the case of children and senior citizens. At the bottom of each illustrated page there is the English name and the Latin name of the fruit or flower portrayed. In addition, every illustration presents a rich web of lines and diverse shapes that stimulates creativity and invites to a relaxing practice of coloring the book.

Other of her books include: *Alice's Adventures in Wonderland. With Original Illustrations by M.C. Iglesias*, *Machiavelli and the Jesuits. An Introduction*, and its Spanish version, *Maquiavelo y los Jesuitas. Una introducción.* Her future projects include illustrated books, volumes on Dante Alighieri, and a novel. In addition, she is the author of all the illustrations that appear on the covers of her books.

To know more about M.C. Iglesias (Clara Iglesias-Rondina) and her work, please visit her websites:
www.mciglesiasart.com (portfolio illustrations)
www.iglesiasrondina.wordpress.com (cv, research interests, publications)
Twitter: www.twitter.com/IglesiasRondina
Facebook: www.facebook.com/pages/MC-Iglesias-Clara-Iglesias-Rondina/1399320866951913

Thank you for coloring!